Eagles

A Buddy Book
by
Julie Murray

VISIT US AT
www.abdopub.com

Published by Buddy Books, an imprint of ABDO Publishing Company, 4940 Viking Drive, Suite 622, Edina, Minnesota 55435. Copyright © 2003 by Abdo Consulting Group, Inc. International copyrights reserved in all countries. No part of this book may be reproduced in any form without written permission from the publisher.

Printed in the United States.

Edited by: Christy DeVillier
Contributing Editors: Matt Ray, Michael P. Goecke
Graphic Design: Maria Hosley
Image Research: Deborah Coldiron
Cover Photograph: Digital Vision Ltd.
Interior Photographs: Digital Stock, Digital Vision Ltd.

Library of Congress Cataloging-in-Publication Data

Murray, Julie, 1969-
  Eagles/Julie Murray.
     p. cm. — (Animal kingdom.)
  Summary: An introduction to the physical characteristics, natural environment, and behavior of eagles.
  ISBN 1-57765-703-9
    1. Eagles—Juvenile literature. [1. Eagles.] I. Title. II. Animal kingdom (Edina, Minn.)

QL696.F32 M867 2002
598.9'42—dc21

2001053609

Contents

Birds Of Prey

Birds of prey are powerful, meat-eating birds. Most birds of prey, or raptors, hunt for their food. All raptors have hooked beaks and sharp claws. A raptor's sharp claws are called talons. Eagles, owls, hawks, vultures, and falcons are all raptors.

Eagles are birds of prey.

Types Of Eagles

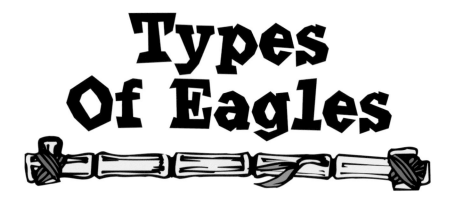

There are about 60 species, or kinds, of eagles. Each eagle species belongs to one of four main eagle groups:

      fish eagles

      snake eagles

      harpy eagles

      booted eagles

African fish eagles

Fish eagles live near water. These eagles mainly eat fish. The bald eagle is one species of fish eagle.

Snake eagles live in Europe, Asia, Africa, and Australia. They feed on snakes, lizards, and other small animals. The bateleur eagle from Africa is a snake eagle.

Some of the biggest eagles are harpy eagles. Harpy eagles live in rain forests. They hunt monkeys and other animals that live in the trees. One species of harpy eagle is the Philippine eagle.

Booted eagles have feathers growing down their legs to their feet. The golden eagle is a booted eagle.

Bald eagle

Golden eagle

Bird Of America

The national bird of the United States is the bald eagle. This North American **raptor** stands for long life, great strength, and freedom. America's bald eagle is on the U.S. national seal. American coins and important U.S. papers show the mighty bald eagle, too.

What They Look Like

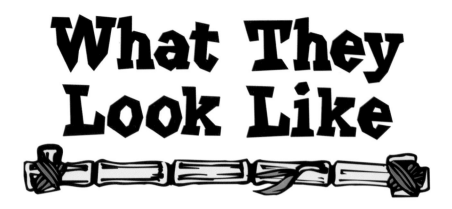

Eagles are different sizes. The martial eagle is the biggest eagle in Africa. This eagle is about 33 inches (84 cm) long. Some harpy eagles are 36 inches (1 m) long.

The Great Nicobar serpent-eagle is one of the smaller eagles. This small eagle is about 16 inches (41 cm) long.

A young martial eagle.

Eagles have strong wings for flying.

A large eagle's outstretched wings can be eight feet (2.4 m) across. Some eagles have **talons** as long as four inches (ten cm).

Where They Live

Eagles live all over the world except in Antarctica. Some eagles stay in one place all year long. **Migrating** eagles move from one place to another as the seasons change.

A young harpy eagle in its eyrie.

Eagles make their nests high up in trees or rocky cliffs. An eagle nest is called an eyrie. Eagles build their eyries with sticks, leaves, and grass.

Many eagles use the same eyrie every year. They will make last year's nest bigger by adding more sticks and grass. So, eagle nests can get very big. People have found eyries that are over nine feet (three m) across!

Hunting And Eating

Eagles mostly hunt during the day. These raptors catch and kill prey with their feet and talons. Eagles eat many kinds of small animals. Fish, ducks, rabbits, mice, and small deer are food for eagles. Sometimes, eagles eat carrion, or dead animals, too. These raptors can eat one pound (0.5 kg) of food in four minutes.

Sharp Eagle Eyes

Eagles and other raptors have excellent eyesight. These birds may see eight times better than people. An eagle can see a rabbit from one mile (1.6 km) away!

Eaglets

A female eagle commonly lays two eggs at a time. One or both eagle parents sit on the eggs to keep them warm. Keeping eggs warm is called incubation. Incubation may last as long as 45 days until the eggs hatch.

A bald eagle feeding its eaglet.

Baby eagles are called eaglets. Eagle parents feed their eaglets bits of meat. At 10 weeks old, these young eagles may be ready to fly. Then, they must learn how to hunt. Some five-month-old eagles can begin living on their own. Eagles can live for more than 20 years.

Important Words

carrion dead animals.

eyrie an eagle's nest.

incubation keeping eggs warm until they
    hatch.

migrate to move from one place to another
    when the seasons change.

prey an animal that is food for another animal.

raptor a large, meat-eating bird with talons
    and a hooked beak.

species living things that are very much alike.

talons the long, hooked claws of raptors.

Web Sites

The Raptor Center

www.raptor.cvm.umn.edu
This educational site features facts, raptor sounds, moving pictures, and rescue stories.

American Bald Eagle Information

www.baldeagleinfo.com
Information on America's national bird, including the famous "Old Abe," can be found here.

Nesting Eagles.com

www.nestingeagles.com/index.htm
Watch live eagles and learn about eagle conservation at this American Eagle Foundation web site.

Index